D0335329

creatures
of the sea

Humpback Whales

Other titles in the series:

creatures of the sea

Humpback Whales

Kris Hirschmann

KIDHAVEN
PRESS™

THOMSON

GALE

San Diego • Detroit • New York • San Francisco • Cleveland
New Haven, Conn. • Waterville, Maine • London • Munich

For more information, contact
KidHaven Press
27500 Drake Rd.
Farmington Hills, MI 48331-3535
Or you can visit our Internet site at http://www.gale.com

LIBRARY OF CONGRESS CATALOGING-IN-PUBLICATION DATA

Hirschmann, Kris, 1967–
  Humpback whales / by Kris Hirschmann.
    p. cm.—(Creatures of the sea)
Summary: Discusses the physical features, environment, eating habits, life
cycle of the humpback whale, as well as the dangers they face and their
unique way of communicating.
Includes bibliographical references and index (p.   ).
  ISBN 0-7377-0984-7 (hardback : alk. paper)
1.Humpback whale—Juvenile literature. [1. Humpback whale. 2. Whales.
3. Endangered species.] I. Title. II. Series.
  QL737 .C424 H57 2003
  599 .5'25—dc21
                                                    2002000459

Printed in the United States of America

Table of Contents

Introduction

To the Edge of Extinction and Back

Humpback whales are among the world's largest—and most impressive—creatures. These "gentle giants," as they are sometimes called, have glided through the earth's oceans for millions of years.

Through most of this period, there were about one hundred thousand to two hundred thousand humpbacks in the world. But in the 1700s, fishermen began to kill humpbacks and other whales for money. They collected and sold the whales' oil, which was used to light lamps. The whales' bony parts, which could be made into combs and other hard objects, were also valuable. Before long whales were used in a large number of items. More whales were killed to meet the growing demand, and the world humpback population began to shrink.

The situation went from bad to worse in the late 1800s. The steam engine made faster boats possible, which made whales easier to hunt. The explosive harpoon made it possible to kill more whales than ever before. Whalers slaughtered vast numbers of humpbacks. By the mid-1900s, just a few thousand humpbacks were left in the world. One of the earth's most incredible creatures was in danger of extinction.

In the 1960s, international laws were written to protect humpbacks and other whales. Commercial whaling did not stop right away, but it did taper off over the next two decades. By the late 1980s, whales were no longer being hunted commercially. With the

A humpback whale slowly swims in the sea. Efforts to save humpbacks began in the 1960s.

whaling threat gone, the humpback population began to increase, and it has been growing ever since. Today, scientists estimate that between seven thousand and ten thousand humpback whales are in the world.

Although the humpback whale is still considered endangered, these animals appear to be making a remarkable comeback. Will the comeback continue? That depends mostly on the health of the world's oceans. If people keep the seas pollution-free, then the humpback whale population will probably continue to grow. With human effort and dedication, these magnificent animals will be around for many millions of years to come.

A Whale of an Animal

Humpback whales belong to the **cetacean** (seh-TAY-shun) family. This family includes all whales, dolphins, and porpoises. Including the humpback, seventy-nine known cetacean species exist.

Averaging forty-five to fifty feet in length and thirty-three tons in weight, humpback whales are among the largest cetaceans. Only four other whale species (blue whales, finback whales, sperm whales, and right whales) are larger.

Humpback Basics

There are three areas of the world where humpback whales live. One population lives in the North Atlantic Ocean, one lives in the North Pacific Ocean, and one ranges from the Antarctic seas to the South Pacific Ocean.

Humpback whales migrate, which means they travel back and forth between different home areas at different times of the year. During the warm summer months, humpbacks can be found in the food-rich waters near the earth's poles. But when winter approaches, the whales head to warmer tropical or subtropical waters (the regions nearest the equator).

Wherever they go, humpback whales are instantly recognizable by their unique diving technique. A humpback arches its body when it is getting ready to dive below the water's surface. The arching action pushes the whale's small dorsal (back) fin up into a humped position. The humpback whale gets its name from this feature.

Humpbacks Are Mammals

Although they live in the water, humpbacks (and all other cetaceans) are not fish. They are mammals. Scientists believe that whales evolved many millions of years ago from land-based animals that became adapted to life in the sea.

Today, humpbacks still share many traits with their land-based ancestors. Female humpbacks give birth to their offspring, as do most other mammals. They produce milk inside their bodies to feed their babies. Also, humpbacks are warm-blooded, which means that their bodies are at a constant temperature of about ninety-seven degrees Fahrenheit. (In contrast, the body temperature of cold-blooded creatures, including fish, changes with the surrounding temperature.)

Because humpbacks spend a lot of time in chilly polar waters, they have some special ways to keep their bodies warm. Each humpback has a six-inch-thick layer of **blubber** (dense fat) just underneath its tough skin. The blubber traps the humpback's body heat. Humpbacks can also open or close blood vessels in their fins to help regulate their body temperature. When the blood vessels are open, heat escapes and the whale cools down. When the vessels are closed, the whale's warm blood stays deeper inside the body, and little heat is lost.

Two humpback whales show off their dorsal fins as they effortlessly arch into the water.

A Breath of Fresh Air

Humpbacks share another important trait with their land-based relatives: They both must breathe air to survive. A humpback breathes through two large nostril-like holes on the top of its head. Together, these nostrils are called the **blowhole**.

A humpback may stay at or near the surface for a long time. During this period, the whale breathes through its blowhole once every two or three minutes. But when the humpback is getting ready to

Air, water vapor, and mucus spray out of a humpback's blowhole as it exhales.

dive, it takes five or six deep breaths in a row. The whale is building up its oxygen supply so it will be comfortable underwater.

After the humpback dives, it holds its breath and uses powerful muscles to keep its blowhole closed. A humpback usually stays underwater between three and twenty-five minutes without breathing. After a while, however, the whale runs out of air. It rises to the surface and exhales, or "blows." Stale air, water vapor, and mucus shoot from the blowhole, creating a misty plume called a **spout**.

A humpback's spout is unique. It has a bushy or balloonlike shape, and it usually rises about ten feet into the air. It is possible to tell whether a blowing whale is a humpback just from the shape of the spout.

Distinctive Features

Humpbacks can also be identified by other characteristics. The humpback's best-known feature is probably its gigantic pectoral (side) fins. Each of these fins can be one-third the length of the entire whale!

The humpback's scientific name, in fact, comes partly from this trait. The humpback is known to scientists as *Megaptera novaeangliae*, which is Latin for "big-winged New Englander." The "big-winged" part of the name comes from the large pectoral fins, which stick out on either side of the whale like slender wings. The "New England" part of the name was adopted because the first ever recorded humpback whale was spotted off the coast of New England.

A humpback can also be recognized by its large, flattened head, which accounts for about one-third of the animal's length. The head is dotted with bumpy knobs called **tubercles**. A stiff hair sticks out of the middle of each tubercle, much as whiskers stick out of a dog's muzzle. No one is sure exactly what the tubercles do, but it is likely that they help the whale to sense its surroundings in some way. Flowing water might wiggle the hairs, for instance, thereby helping the humpback to feel and judge ocean currents.

A humpback cruises through the water by moving its large pectoral fins.

A humpback whale's fluke, or tail, is easily identified by its black-and-white markings.

Standing Out from the Crowd

Features such as tubercles and pectoral fins make it easy to tell humpbacks apart from other species of whales. But individual whales have their own unique markings.

Each humpback whale has a pattern of black-and-white markings on the underside of its broad tail fin, which is called a **fluke**. A diving humpback briefly lifts its fluke above the water, exposing the pattern underneath. Although the moment is short, it is long enough to give a human observer a good look at the whale's markings. No two fluke patterns are alike, just as no two human fingerprints are alike.

Scientists who study whales use these markings to identify individuals. They can learn about humpbacks' migration and birth patterns, monitor the worldwide humpback population, and much more.

chapter 2

Amazing Eaters

Despite their enormous size, humpback whales eat some of the ocean's tiniest creatures. They survive on a diet of krill (small shrimplike creatures), plankton, and small fish.

A humpback needs plenty of "fuel" to power its gigantic body. To get the energy it needs, a big humpback may consume up to three thousand pounds of krill and fish in a single day! That is a lot of food. But finding a meal is no problem for humpback whales, which have many ways to catch all the food they need.

Baleen Whales

Humpbacks are **baleen** whales. This means that instead of teeth, their mouths contain hundreds of plates of baleen, which is a hard substance similar to human fingernails. The outer edge of each baleen plate is smooth. The inner edge is fringed to form a kind of natural net inside the humpback's mouth. Water can pass through the baleen net, but solid food such as fish and krill cannot.

There are eleven species of baleen whales. Of these, six (including the humpback) are also called **rorquals**. Rorquals have pleated undersides that can expand like an accordion to hold huge quantities of water. A typical humpback has about twenty pleats.

A humpback explodes out of the water to catch food. Baleen bristles (inset) keep food in a whale's mouth as water is pushed out.

These pleats allow a feeding humpback to gulp a volume of water much larger than its own head. More water usually means more food, so an expandable whale can capture more prey in each mouthful.

When a humpback wants to eat, it opens its huge mouth wide and takes in a bunch of fish or krill along with a giant mouthful of seawater. The humpback then closes its mouth, trapping the prey inside, and uses its powerful tongue to force the seawater out through the baleen. When all of the water is gone, the humpback swallows any small animals that remain inside the mouth.

Hunting with Bubbles

A humpback does not simply swim along with its mouth open, waiting for food to be washed inside. Humpbacks hunt, and they use some amazing tricks to round up their prey.

The humpback's best-known hunting technique is called **bubble netting**. Starting about fifty to one hundred feet below the water's surface, a humpback swims around a school of fish in a slow upward spiral. As it swims, the humpback releases a steady stream of bubbles from its blowhole. The rising bubbles create a glittering, moving curtain that confuses the fish and makes them squeeze into a tight ball. When the fish are packed close together, the humpback opens its huge mouth and lunges upward through the school. This method allows a humpback to catch thousands of fish in one mighty gulp.

A wall of bubbles (as shown here) can confuse a whale's prey and cause them to gather close together.

Another common hunting technique is called the **bubble cloud**. In this technique, a humpback blows air from its mouth to create a large cloud of bubbles. The bubble cloud confuses the whale's prey and probably also hides the approaching whale. By the time the humpback appears, it is too late for the prey to escape.

Other Techniques

Bubble netting and bubble clouds are the humpback's most common hunting techniques. But other methods are used from time to time.

One alternative hunting method is called **lobtail feeding**. To use this method, a humpback goes into a dive near a school of fish. As the whale descends, it smacks the surface of the water with its powerful tail, stunning the school of fish. The humpback then blows a bubble cloud, swims toward its prey, and sucks fish into its open mouth.

Humpbacks work together to capture their prey by using the group-hunting method, as shown here.

A humpback may also go into a deep dive to look for food. But this behavior is rare. Most of the animals eaten by humpbacks live near the surface, so deep hunting dives are usually a waste of time. Also, humpbacks spend most of their lives in coastal waters that are only a few hundred feet deep. A whale cannot dive too far in such shallow seas.

Group Hunting

Sometimes humpback whales hunt in packs. Several humpbacks gather and cooperate to blow an especially large bubble net or bubble cloud. Then all of the whales lunge simultaneously at the trapped prey. Sometimes the whales erupt out of the water together, head first, with their mouths wide open and their pleats fully extended. This amazing display is one of the most awe-inspiring sights in nature!

The number of humpbacks hunting together probably depends on the amount of food available. If a school of fish is just large enough to feed one humpback, then only one whale will hunt that school. Meanwhile other whales in the same area will wander away in different directions, looking for food on their own. If a school of fish is big enough to feed more than one whale, however, then nearby humpbacks will swim over to help with the hunt. Usually just two or three whales hunt together, but many more may gather if there is an unusually large amount of food. For example, in 1989 millions of small fish gathered off the New England coast. Huge numbers of humpbacks gathered to enjoy the feast. Hunting groups of twenty or more humpbacks were seen at this time.

Feast or Famine

A humpback's feeding behavior changes with the seasons. During the summer, humpbacks hunt almost all the time. They gorge themselves with food and become bigger and stronger. It takes about ten pounds of food to create one pound of whale, so a humpback must eat a great deal in order to continue growing.

But the effort is important. When autumn arrives, humpbacks begin the long journey to their tropical winter homes. They depend on the blubber they have built up over the food-rich summer months to give them enough energy to make this trip. Also, although scientists do not know why, humpbacks do not eat at all during the winter months. So during this time, a thick blubber layer is a humpback's only insurance against starvation.

A humpback loses much of its body mass during the winter. In the spring, however, the whale starts swimming toward its summer home. Before long the humpback is back in fertile waters, and it will start the feeding cycle all over again.

chapter

3

The Yearly Cycle

Humpback whales enjoy fairly long lives. Most humpbacks live between forty and fifty years. A particularly healthy humpback may live even longer.

Throughout its life, a humpback follows a predictable yearly cycle. Late spring, summer, and early autumn are the humpback's feeding times. The rest of the year is devoted to migration, mating, and giving birth to baby whales—activities essential to the survival of the species.

Migration

During the warm months of the year, humpbacks live far above or below the equator. Food is plentiful in the cooler ocean regions during the summertime, so the whales gorge themselves every day for months. They live in harmony with each other, and they grow fat and content.

23

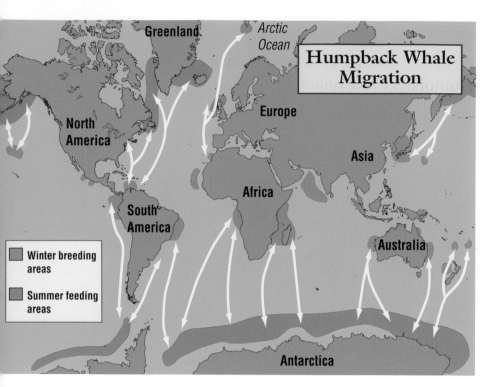

Greenland

Arctic Ocean

Humpback Whale Migration

Europe

North America

Asia

Africa

South America

Australia

Winter breeding areas

Summer feeding areas

Antarctica

When autumn arrives, however, humpbacks become restless. Chemical changes in their bodies tell them that it is time to seek their winter ranges. One by one, the whales swim away from the waters that have been their home for the past several months. Northern humpbacks head south. Southern humpbacks do just the opposite: They must swim north to reach warmer waters.

Migration distances vary. Some humpbacks migrate just a few hundred miles, but such a short journey is rare. Most humpbacks travel thousands of miles to reach their winter homes.

On the Way

As it journeys, a humpback uses its powerful tail to push itself through the water. The whale travels at a steady speed of three to four miles per hour, never stopping to eat. It does not stop to sleep, either. Humpbacks rest only half of their brain at any time, leaving the other half fully awake. The awake part of the brain keeps the whale swimming toward its destination twenty-four hours a day.

During its migration (and at other times of the year as well), a humpback occasionally leaps out of the water. This behavior is called **breaching**. A breaching

A humpback whale puts on a magnificent show as it gracefully breaches.

humpback pumps its tail to thrust itself upward. With its enormous body almost fully out of the water, the humpback twists around. Then it falls back-first into the ocean with a mighty splash that can be seen for miles around.

There are several reasons that humpbacks breach. Barnacles and other parasites often grow on the whale's skin, and breaching helps shake them off. Breaching also seems to be a form of play or because they are excited. And humpbacks may leap from the water just because they feel like it.

A humpback may also slap its tail fluke or its pectoral fins against the water's surface. Slapping the tail is called **lobtailing**; slapping the pectoral fins is called **flippering**. The slaps make sharp noises that can be heard from a great distance underwater. These noises might be one way a humpback communicates with other whales.

Mating Season

It takes about a month for most humpbacks to reach their winter homes. Once they arrive, mating season begins.

During mating season, female humpbacks are the center of attention. Wherever they swim, they are surrounded by hopeful males. As few as three or as many as twenty male humpbacks court a single female. One of these males stays very close to the female and is called the "principal escort." The other males sometimes become aggressive and attack the principal

A male humpback (right) gently approaches a female in hopes of mating with her.

escort. They hope to chase him away so they can take his place by the female's side.

After a while, one male will succeed in mating with the female. It will take almost a year for a baby to develop inside the female. During that year, the female will make two more migrations—a return trip to her summer feeding ground, and then another migration to her winter home. The year after she mates, the female will give birth to her baby (called a calf) in the same waters where she became pregnant.

Most female humpbacks switch back and forth between mating and calving. They mate one year, then have a calf the next year, then mate again the following year, and so on. Most female humpbacks calve once every two years.

Taking Care of Baby

No one has ever seen a humpback whale give birth. But it is likely that the calf emerges tail first. If it came out head first, the calf could drown during the birth process. Once it is born, however, the calf is in no danger of drowning. It is a natural swimmer. Nudged by its mother, the brand-new whale rises to the water's surface to take its first breath.

A newborn humpback is an impressive animal. At birth, the calf is already fourteen feet long and weighs

A humpback calf (top) swims hard to keep up with its mother.

about fifteen hundred pounds. The enormous infant swims close to its mother's side, surfacing often to breathe. The mother swims more slowly than usual so her calf can keep up. Still, the baby must wave its tail furiously to match its mother's pace.

For the first six months of its life, a humpback calf feeds on milk produced by its mother. The milk comes from two mammary glands that are found near the tail, on the underside of the body. The glands are hidden inside slits. The calf pokes a slit with its head to expose the mother's nipple and start the milk flowing.

Humpback milk is very rich. It may be as much as 40 percent fat. (In comparison, cow's milk is 4 percent fat, and human milk is 2 percent fat.) A hungry humpback calf drinks one hundred gallons of this fattening fluid every day! As a result, the calf grows quickly, gaining as much as fifty pounds in a single day. By the time the calf is six months old, it will have doubled its length.

Return Migration

When spring arrives, humpbacks set out on the long journey to their summer waters. The whales have not eaten all winter, so they are hungry. The foodless months have taken an especially severe toll on calving females, some of which have lost one-third of their body weight. All of the whales will eat as they migrate, working to build up the bulk they have lost.

For males and newly pregnant females, the migration is just a long swim. For females with calves, the journey is slower and more difficult. The mother humpback looks after her baby and watches for dangerous sharks and killer whales. These predators seldom attack adult humpbacks, but they sometimes go after an unprotected calf.

Calves Learn Skills

The poleward migration is a calf's real introduction to the humpback way of life. During the journey, the calf practices adult behaviors like breaching and lobtailing. It becomes bigger, stronger, and more confident. It also learns the migration route. For the rest of its life, a whale will travel back and forth between the regions it "inherits" from its mother.

By late spring, all of the humpbacks have reached their summer grounds. Feeding once again becomes the most important activity in the whales' lives. The infants learn this important skill from their mothers. Within about six months the calves will be able to catch their own food. The young whales will stay with their mothers a while longer, but they usually strike out on their own when they are about a year old. Mother and baby may see each other again—or they may not. That is the way of life in the sea.

chapter

4

Singers of the Seas

Humpback whales have one trait for which they are famous around the world. They sing! At certain times of the year, male humpbacks fill the oceans with eerie moans, grunts, and squeals that can be heard for miles around.

Humpbacks are not the only singing animals. Some insects, amphibians, and many birds sing, too. But these creatures' simple songs cannot compare to the humpback's magnificent melodies. The humpback has the most complex—and perhaps the most beautiful—song of any animal on Earth.

Making the Song

Humpbacks seldom sing during the summer months. During the winter, however, they sing almost constantly. They fill the waters with all sorts of noises that can exceed 170 decibels, which is nearly as

A humpback whale sings underwater. Its song can be heard for miles.

loud as a rocket launch. Above the water, the whale songs are very faint. But underwater, the humpback's cries are loud enough to travel up to twenty miles—and certain parts of the whale's song might travel even farther. Some scientists believe that a humpback's deepest notes can be heard all the way across the ocean.

A humpback's song can be broken down into distinct chunks called **themes**. There are usually five to eight different themes in a song. A humpback sings the same themes in the same order every time. The entire song may take just a few minutes to complete, or it may take as much as half an hour. When the whale finishes the song, it goes back to the beginning and starts again. A humpback sometimes sings its song over and over for days on end without stopping.

Sometimes many humpbacks sing at once. They do not sing the same notes at the same time, however. Each whale sings at its own pace, making no attempt to harmonize with its neighbors.

All Together Now

Although humpbacks do not sing in unison, they *are* singing the same tune. All of the whales in any area learn a common song. Humpbacks throughout the North Pacific, for example, will sing the same song,

Whales that live together in one area are able to sing the same song.

no matter how far apart they live. Humpbacks living in the South Pacific also have a consistent song—but it is a different song from the one heard in the north. Northern and southern humpbacks do not mix, so they never have a chance to learn each other's melodies.

Perhaps the most amazing thing about the humpbacks' song is how it changes over time. The whales all sing a certain song at the beginning of the winter. But during the season, the song changes a little bit here and there. These little changes eventually add up to big changes. By the time winter ends, the whales' song sounds completely different than it did a few months earlier. And yet somehow all of the humpbacks are still singing the same song. Even if they are

Water cascades from a humpback's fluke as it dives under the ocean's surface.

Two friendly humpback whales join together in song.

separated by great distances, humpbacks manage to keep up with the changes and learn the new tune.

When the humpbacks start the journey to their summer territories, they stop singing. But the song is not forgotten. The whales remember their song for many months, until they return again to their winter range. Then they pick up right where they left off. The song is the same one the humpbacks were singing at the end of the previous winter. But it will not stay the same for long. By the time the new season ends, the song once again will be completely different.

Singing for a Reason

So why do humpbacks sing? Although there is no proven connection, scientists believe that the singing has something to do with the whales' mating patterns. They believe this mostly because only male humpbacks sing, and only during mating season. When male birds, frogs, and insects sing, they are trying to attract mates. It makes sense that the humpback's song would serve the same purpose.

It is also possible that humpbacks sing to communicate with each other. The whale's song probably does not contain actual messages, as spoken words do. But a humpback might very well sing to mark its territory, advertise its presence, or simply show off its powerful voice. These meanings are

A singing whale approaches a research boat holding a crew that is recording the whale's tunes.

not understood by humans, but other whales hear them loud and clear.

Some people think humpbacks sing for another reason. They believe that humpback whales sing to express their joy at being alive. Although no scientific evidence supports this belief, it is not hard to understand why people might think this way. Humpbacks *do* leap when they are happy and excited. Their songs could be seen as an outward expression of the same joyful inner state.

Human Fascination

Whatever its purpose, the humpback's song is awe-inspiring. As long as people have walked the earth, they have been amazed and fascinated by the humpback whale's yearly serenade.

Until recently, people had to go to the sea to hear humpbacks singing. But the invention of underwater recording equipment changed that. Using special microphones, scientists have been able to record whale songs. These recordings have made their way into many land-based labs, where they have been used in the scientific study of humpback whales. The recordings have also made their way onto CDs that are available to the public. So people today do not have to be near the ocean to hear the song of the humpbacks. They can listen to a recording in the comfort of their own homes.

Some people have taken their interest in the humpback's song one step further. They have used

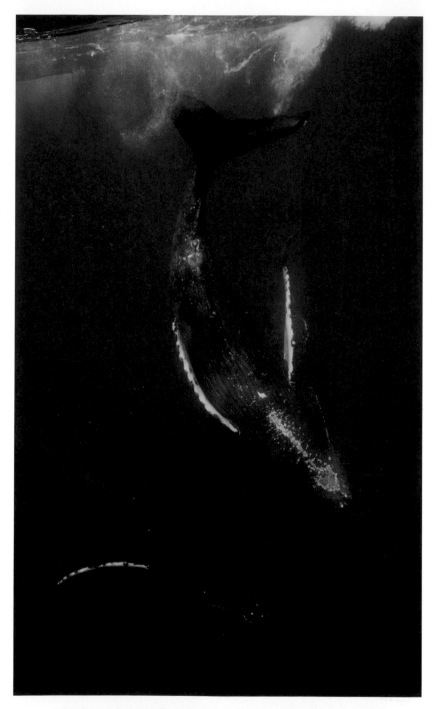

Two whales plunge back into the ocean from a dive.

these sounds in human music! There are many songs and even some symphonies that include humpback noises. Compositions such as these are just one more sign of humankind's ongoing fascination with the mighty humpback whale.

Perhaps the humpbacks' greatest honor occurred in 1977, when two Voyager spacecraft blasted off from the earth and headed toward the edge of the solar system. The vehicles carried recordings of many Earth sounds, including singing humpbacks. It is appropriate that the humpbacks' song was part of this historic recording. Through their singing, humpback whales add a special touch of beauty and mystery to the planet. They also help to make this world unique. No collection of "Earth's greatest hits" would be complete without the song of the magnificent humpback whale.

Glossary

baleen: Bony plates inside the mouths of some whales.

blowhole: The whale's nostrils, located on top of the head.

blubber: Whale fat.

breaching: Leaping out of the water.

bubble cloud: A burst of air blown from the humpback's mouth to confuse prey.

bubble netting: A hunting technique that involves trapping fish in a "net" made of bubbles.

cetacean: The name of the family to which all whales, dolphins, and porpoises belong.

flippering: Slapping the pectoral fins on the water's surface.

fluke: The tail fin.

lobtail feeding: A hunting technique that involves stunning fish with a blow from the tail.

lobtailing: Slapping the tail fluke on the water's surface.

rorqual: Any whale that has a pleated, expandable underside.

spout: The visible plume created when a humpback exhales.

theme: One part of a humpback's song.

tubercles: Bumpy sensory knobs on a humpback's head.

For Further Exploration

Books

Robert F. Baldwin, *New England Whaler*. Minneapolis: Lerner, 1996. In this book, the author shares the rich details of life aboard the square-rigged ships that carried American whale hunters across the world's oceans.

Mark Carwardine, Mason Weinrich, and Peter Evans, *Whales, Dolphins, and Porpoises*. New York: DK, 1998. This book contains hundreds of magnificent photos and illustrations, plus lots of facts about the cetaceans of the world.

Nick Leach and John Gattuso, *Whale Watching (Discovery Travel Adventures)*. New York: Discovery Communications, 1999. Includes all the information you need to plan a whale-watching adventure anywhere in the Northern Hemisphere.

Jim Murphy, *Gone A-Whaling: The Lure of the Sea and the Hunt for the Great Whale*. New York: Clarion Books, 1998. Diary entries form the backbone of this fascinating look at whale hunting in America, from the nineteenth century to today.

Robert Siegel, *Whalesong*. San Francisco: Harper-SanFrancisco, 1991. This book is the fictional tale of Hruna the humpback whale and his journey through life.

Websites

Virtual Whales (www.cs.sfu.ca). This site has movie and sound clips, plus animations of humpback feeding behavior.

A Visual Guide to Humpback Whale Behaviors (www.hwrf.org). Includes great pictures of humpbacks breaching, lobtailing, and performing other typical behaviors.

Wild Whales: Humpback Whale (www.wildwhales. org). Scroll all the way to the bottom of the page for a recording of the humpback's song.

Index

picture credits

Cover photo: © Michio Hoshino/Minden
   Pictures
© A.N.T./Photo Researchers, 32
© Bacon, Marian/Animals/Animals/Earth
   Scenes, 17
© Corel Corporation, 11, 20
DigitalStock, 7, 14
© Mitsuaki Iwago/Minden Pictures, 25
© Japack Company/CORBIS, 28
© Minden Pictures, 38
© Amos Nachoum/CORBIS, 12
© Flip Nicklin/Minden Pictures, 19, 27, 35, 36
   (Photos obtained under NMFS permit #987.)
Brandy Noon, 24
© Roger Tidman/CORBIS, 17 (inset)
© Kennan Ward/CORBIS, 33, 34
© Stuart Westmorland/CORBIS, 15

about the author

Kris Hirschmann has written more than sixty books for children, mostly on science and nature topics. She is the president of The Wordshop, a business that provides a wide variety of writing and editorial services. She holds a bachelor's degree in psychology from Dartmouth College in Hanover, New Hampshire. Hirschmann lives just outside of Orlando, Florida, with her husband, Michael.